EFFIN' BIRDS

EFFIN' BIRDS

A Field Guide to Identification

FACK

Aaron Reynolds

TEN SPEED PRESS
California | New York

To my mother-in-law, who does not
believe that this is an acceptable way
to make a living

Introduction

HAVE YOU EVER listened to the melodic chirping of birds and wondered what they were trying to communicate?

Some of the world's most brilliant scientists have spent decades studying birdsong to gain an understanding of birds: their society, their needs, their hopes and dreams. Are birds gripped by the paralysing fear that they'll fail to provide for their families? Do they aspire to meaningful careers? Are they frustrated at the pace of social progress in the world?

It turns out that these were the feelings of the scientists and not the birds at all. Advances in machine learning over the past ten years have allowed for detailed scenario analysis of birds and their songs, and multiple computer-driven studies* that compiled years' worth of audio and video recordings came to an astonishing conclusion: most of the time, birds are just saying, "Fuck off."

Sometimes they're saying fuck off to predators. Sometimes to other birds. In the studies, scientists found that the birds were

---

* I made these up because this book is fake – but keep that as a secret between you and me and the handful of other nerds who read footnotes.

disproportionately saying fuck off to the scientists studying them, which led to some sober re-examination of their bird-handling protocols.

This astonishing breakthrough has led to re-evaluations of historic recordings, including one analysis that showed US President Lyndon B. Johnson's pet lovebirds telling British Prime Minister Harold Wilson to "fuck off and keep fucking off until your feet get wet" during a White House visit, and another in which Challenger the Bald Eagle told Major League Baseball Commissioner Bud Selig to "find a newer and more interesting way to fuck off" at the 1998 World Series. Most embarrassingly, computer analysis shows that the pigeons in the "Feed the Birds" scene of *Mary Poppins* are actually saying, "Just give us the fucking bread before we die of old age."

While it would prove impossible to create a definitive listing of every way birds say fuck off, this book is an attempt to catalogue some of the most common, and to place them into broader societal context, along with identifying bird behaviours and characteristics. And while very few people will have access to the advanced computational power needed to understand birdsong precisely, the hope is that the knowledge contained in this book will allow you to look directly into a bird's eyes and understand it when it tells you to fuck off with that shit.

FUCK
OFF
WITH
THAT
SHIT

Part One

LAND BIRDS

Contrary to popular belief, land birds are not flightless birds – they are birds that you don't generally find hanging out on the lake. As such, they have a contrasting set of complaints: where a water bird is likely to advise a vacationer on a boogie board to fuck off back to the city, a land bird would more frequently tell a cable repair person to fuck off out of their tree – two completely different sentiments.

FUCK ALL THE WAY OFF

DIRT CHICKEN

Low to the ground and generally silent, the dirt chicken kicks up a ruckus when stepped on or tripped over.

HABITAT: Underfoot.

IDENTIFYING CHARACTERISTICS: An inability to share blame; repeated behaviours that lead to the same undesired results.

IF YOU HAVE A POINT, I WOULD LOVE FOR YOU TO FUCKING GET TO IT

PEEVISH RINGNECK

This is a bird that has heard one too many stories and has other shit to get done.

HABITAT: Always on the go between places.

IDENTIFYING CHARACTERISTICS: Rolling eyes and a lot of passive-aggressive sighing noises.

WHY DO YOU THINK I CARE ABOUT THIS?

IS IT THE FUCKING WEEKEND YET?

FOR FUCK'S SAKE

LIGHT-BELLIED DEFEATIST

This bird's frustrated cry is so compelling that the National Society of Pessimists put the light-bellied defeatist on their coat of arms.

HABITAT: Wherever it has nested, it is not good enough.

IDENTIFYING CHARACTERISTICS: Furrowed brow, high blood pressure.

I'M JUST GONNA GET INTO BED AND EAT A WHOLE FUCKING PIE

CAPITULATION FINCH

When the world is too much to handle, the capitulation finch has a nap.

HABITAT: In bed, on the couch, lying on the floor between the bed and the couch.

IDENTIFYING CHARACTERISTICS: Sweatpants.

CONGRATULATIONS ON
SCALING SHIT MOUNTAIN

YOUR
PRIORITIES
ARE FUCKED

FUCK YOU, I'M NOT SORRY

INCOMPUNCTIOUS OWL

This owl's large size and dominating personality allow it to do basically anything it wants.

HABITAT: Wherever it wants to go.

IDENTIFYING CHARACTERISTICS: An alarming lack of empathy.

FUCK YOUR EXCUSES

COME BACK
WHEN YOU
GET YOUR SHIT
TOGETHER

KINGSFIELD'S VULTURE

No animal has ever prevailed in a confrontation with
a kingsfield's vulture.

HABITAT: Educational institutions, usually the kind with gargoyles.

IDENTIFYING CHARACTERISTICS: A steely, emotionless gaze while you
attempt to explain why you're handing in this paper so late.

I AM SUFFERING FROM BULLSHIT FATIGUE

WEARY JACKDAW

A small, vocal bird with an overdeveloped outrage muscle.

HABITAT: Twitter, Facebook, whatever is next.

IDENTIFYING CHARACTERISTICS: Despite being horrified and mentally spent, the weary jackdaw is unable to stop browsing social media.

WHY DID I COME TO WORK TODAY?

FUZZY CHATTERER

You finally got on a roll at the office: you're being productive, you're pleased with your work, and you're feeling good about your contribution to the team. Then, like an Eeyore-shaped cloud, the fuzzy chatterer arrives.

HABITAT: Some dark corner of your workplace.

IDENTIFYING CHARACTERISTICS: A sense of imminent doom that the chatterer passes along like the common cold.

YOU ARE
THE WORST
FUCKING
HUMAN

WHO'S IN
CHARGE OF
THIS FUCKING
TRAIN WRECK?

GET THE FUCK
OVER YOURSELF

ONEROUS OSPREY

The most ironic aspect of the onerous osprey is the high regard it holds for itself while denigrating others for the high regard they hold for themselves. Naturally, this irony is lost on them.

HABITAT: Commonly found in the "eight items or less" line at the supermarket with sixteen items, complaining about the person in front of them with nine items.

IDENTIFYING CHARACTERISTICS: Slightly downy feathers, an unyielding gaze, and a completely incomprehensible value system.

I'M NOT STICKING
AROUND TO SEE HOW
THIS SHIT ENDS

THAT'S A LOT OF BULLSHIT FOR A SMALL MAN

HUMPBACKED SPARROW

This incredibly tiny bird makes a lot of noise despite its size.

HABITAT: Hiding behind a username that's a random word and a four-digit number.

IDENTIFYING CHARACTERISTICS: Types in all uppercase, can't read past a headline, and is invested in only one thing: "winning."

IT APPEARS THAT I OVERESTIMATED THE FUCK OUT OF YOUR INTELLIGENCE

MOTHER WREN

The mother wren gives every one of her hatchlings the benefit of the doubt until it is far too late.

HABITAT: A cozy, suburban home that is simultaneously filled with warm nostalgia and the unrelenting horror of Formica.

IDENTIFYING CHARACTERISTICS: Every conversation with a mother wren eventually turns into a judgmental diatribe on why you can't afford to buy a house.

WHAT IN THE FUCK IS MY LIFE?

HAVE SOME FUCKING DIGNITY

THANKS A LOT, FUCKSTAIN

AGGRO RAVEN

A shiny bird with a pointed beak that delivers cutting evaluations of your personality, manner of dress, and ability to function in society.

HABITAT: For whatever reason, there's always one in your circle of friends.

IDENTIFYING CHARACTERISTICS: A pyromaniacal zest for burning bridges.

GET SOME FUCKING POPCORN, IT'S SHITSHOW TIME

COLLARED OBSERVER PENGUIN

Thriving on the conflict of other birds, the collared observer penguin spends its time watching – and occasionally instigating – fights that it refuses to participate in.

HABITAT: Always the sidelines, never the fray.

IDENTIFYING CHARACTERISTICS: A black hole of emptiness where others would have values.

I AM A GODDAMNED DELIGHT

TALKING TO YOU IS FUCKING EXHAUSTING

TODAY IS INTERNATIONAL STOP BEING A FUCKFACE DAY

CANTANKEROUS REDWING

This bird is strongly attracted to irritants like noise, modern fashion trends, and the expression of joy.

HABITAT: You cannot avoid the cantankerous redwing, especially at parties.

IDENTIFYING CHARACTERISTICS: A militaristic lack of fun.

WHO PUT THESE DUMBFUCKS IN CHARGE?

DISAVOWAL PHEASANT

This pheasant resides in a world where it has no responsibility for the state of things.

HABITAT: Previously found in the endless headers of a forwarded email chain, but has more recently been spotted on Facebook.

IDENTIFYING CHARACTERISTICS: Highly amplified outrage and a willingness to believe memes.

YOU'RE A FUCKING DISGRACE TO NEPOTISM

TINY HORNBEAK

The tiny hornbeak will never get a promotion while the boss still has unemployed nephews.

HABITAT: Often found sulking in a cubicle near the back where the fluorescent tubes are flickering.

IDENTIFYING CHARACTERISTICS: The large ears and weak chin of one whose parents believed in keeping things in the family.

OWN
YOUR
BULLSHIT

THAT'S A
MASSIVE FUCKING
OVERREACTION

THIS SHIT MAKES ME TIRED

FUCK OFF,
I'M READING

OH YEAH, FUCK ALL OF THAT SHIT

PINK JOINER

The pink joiner is somewhat poorly named, as it is not a joiner. It is also not pink.

HABITAT: Wherever activities are announced, pink joiners will be there to belittle them.

IDENTIFYING CHARACTERISTICS: An air of above-it-all aloofness used to disguise the fact that it is basically not good at anything.

LET ME GUESS: YOU'RE A FUCKING DIMWIT

SPECKLED ARBITER

The arbiter family of birds prefer to perch very high in trees, where they are ideally placed to look down on everyone.

HABITAT: Often found on horses – the taller the better.

IDENTIFYING CHARACTERISTICS: The speckled arbiter is most easily recognised by its belief that it alone is qualified to judge what should be considered *Star Trek*.

WHY ARE YOU ARGUING WITH REALITY?

UNEQUIVOCAL EAGLE

This eagle perceives the world in high-contrast monochrome
and is only able to identify simple shapes.

HABITAT: Reddit.

IDENTIFYING CHARACTERISTICS: Absurdly literal, unable to recognise
rhetorical questions, and willing to believe any information
presented in a graph or pie chart.

I NEED A FUCKING NAP

FUCK-A-DOODLE-DOO

I DIDN'T UNDERSTAND YOUR ARGUMENT BECAUSE IT'S BULLSHIT

MOTHERRRRR FUCKERRRRR

ARTICULATE CROW

This bird is loud as fuck.

FUCK OFF

WRATHFUL SPARROW

This tiny bird has a narrow emotional range, from irate to choleric. Keep your distance unless you want to get pecked.

HABITAT: Generally makes its home in a place that will surely cause it to lose its shit, like the comment section of an online newspaper.

IDENTIFYING CHARACTERISTICS: Marked by strong red colouration and steam blowing out of its ears.

I AM FUCKING MAGNIFICENT

VAINGLORIOUS GREBE

When you lock eyes with a vainglorious grebe, you find yourself filled with doubts and concerns. Are you underdressed? Will it demand to see your invitation? Do you really belong here?

HABITAT: Found only in the most elegant of forests, the vainglorious grebe prefers to nest in imported designer fabrics.

IDENTIFYING CHARACTERISTICS: Brilliant colours, massive sunglasses.

HOW ABOUT I JUST DO YOUR FUCKING JOB FOR YOU?

VOCATIONAL TERN

The vocational tern isn't here to make things better; the vocational tern is here to entertain itself.

HABITAT: Most frequently found at the part of the meeting where everything goes to shit.

IDENTIFYING CHARACTERISTICS: Smaller vocational terns are passive-aggressive, whereas larger ones are simply aggressive; sometimes it can be hard to tell the two apart.

BY GOD, YOU'RE A DUMB MOTHERFUCKER

FLABBERGAST'S FINCH

The flabbergast's finch expects the best of everyone,
even when there is no evidence that it should expect anything
other than the worst.

HABITAT: Generally found in the orbit of people who will
only disappoint.

IDENTIFYING CHARACTERISTICS: An unusual capacity for surprise.

I WOULD PAY REAL MONEY FOR YOU TO FUCK OFF

FRACTIOUS QUAIL

If you find yourself having angered a fractious quail, the best advice would be to run for as long as you can in any direction without looking back.

HABITAT: Keep running! Don't look back!

IDENTIFYING CHARACTERISTICS: A very sharp beak – Christ, that hurts. Why did you stop running?

LOOK AT THIS GODDAMN TURD FARM

I NEED COFFEE

HOW LONG UNTIL THE FUCKING APOCALYPSE?

FATALISTIC FALCON

Like a giant rain cloud or a swarm of killer bees, the fatalistic falcon darkens the horizon as it approaches.

HABITAT: It doesn't matter, we're all doomed.

IDENTIFYING CHARACTERISTICS: Aware that the end is near, the fatalistic falcon can be heard sighing heavily and dragging its feet.

DO NOT TRY

FUCK
WEEKDAYS

YES, I WANT TO HEAR ALL ABOUT YOUR BULLSHIT

GREY-WINGED ENABLER

It is unclear what the motives of the grey-winged enabler are, but its impact is easy to assess: it draws out the worst instincts in everyone it encounters.

HABITAT: At the bar, encouraging just one more drink.

IDENTIFYING CHARACTERISTICS: It is somehow immune to any negative impacts of its behaviour.

THIS SHIT IS TOO MUCH EVEN FOR ME

ABDICATING SPARROW

When the going gets tough, this hardy little bird fucks off out of self-preservation.

HABITAT: Prefers to nest in low-bullshit areas.

IDENTIFYING CHARACTERISTICS: Hard to tell what it looks like from the front.

I'M A BIG DEAL ON THE FUCKING INTERNET

BEGUILED SWIFT

The beguiled swift's casual Instagram self-portrait has been art-directed by a professional and retouched to within an inch of its life: clearly this bird is an Influencer.

HABITAT: When it isn't buried beak-first in its smartphone, the beguiled swift is tapping away at its computer.

IDENTIFYING CHARACTERISTICS: Frequent talk of metrics, engagement, CPM, ratio, Alexa rank, Klout score, and other things that are clearly not real.

I LIKE YOU
BETTER WHEN
YOU SHUT THE
FUCK UP

IF I WANTED ADVICE
FROM AN ASSHOLE, I
WOULD HAVE ASKED
ON THE INTERNET

YOU ARE CORDIALLY INVITED TO SNIFF MY BUTTHOLE

INDECOROUS GULL

The indecorous gull has abandoned all attempts to participate in polite society but can't quite understand why its party invitations have dried up.

HABITAT: It tries to nest where all the other birds are but is constantly rebuffed. It naturally sees this as a failing of the other birds.

IDENTIFYING CHARACTERISTICS: If you ask the indecorous gull, the problem is definitely society and not the thing where it is always being an asshole.

LOOK, ASSHOLE, I DON'T HAVE TIME TO EXPLAIN

BASICALLY, YOU'RE FUCKING INCOMPETENT

ASTUTE OWL

As much as you don't want an astute owl to be correct,
the astute owl is correct.

HABITAT: Lurking nearby whenever you make a mistake.

IDENTIFYING CHARACTERISTICS: An unnerving sense of timing.

STUFF THAT IN YOUR GARBAGE HOLE

LONG-LEGGED PANACEA

The long-legged panacea has no time for your
poorly researched opinion.

HABITAT: Let's be honest—you're only at the receiving end of this
bird's wrath because you tweeted a garbage reply at it.

IDENTIFYING CHARACTERISTICS: Extreme height that lends extra
authoritative weight to all of its pronouncements.

HOW HAVE
YOU SURVIVED SO
MANY YEARS
OF BEING
AN IMBECILE?

THAT
WAS THE
STUPIDEST

LEAVE THIS TO THE FUCKING PROFESSIONALS

FALLACY'S BLACKBIRD

Whenever conversations requiring expertise and nuance occur, fallacy's blackbird is there to muddy the waters.

HABITAT: Academia, panel shows, letters to the editor.

IDENTIFYING CHARACTERISTICS: Hubris, misplaced confidence, and a history of embarrassing deleted tweets.

WHEN DID I GET SO FUCKING OLD?

CONVERSANT OWL

One day, the conversant owl woke up and realised that it was focused on the wrong parts of life.

HABITAT: On eBay, trying to buy back its childhood.

IDENTIFYING CHARACTERISTICS: Profound sadness for the passing of an era that probably never existed.

FUCK IT, I'M NOT COOKING DINNER

ENERVATED EAGLE

These birds (and their soul-crushing day jobs) keep chain restaurants in business.

HABITAT: A cubicle, being drained of their vitality for too many hours of the day, and then going home to do laundry.

IDENTIFYING CHARACTERISTICS: Unread books, abandoned hobbies, and a Netflix queue that only grows.

NO FUCKING WAY

WHAT THE FUCK IS HAPPENING RIGHT NOW?

OF COURSE YOU DIDN'T PLAN FOR THIS FUCKING CATASTROPHE

FORETHOUGHT'S HERON

When things have gone horribly wrong, you hear the distant call of the forethought's heron: "I tollllld you sooooooo."

HABITAT: Never to be found in the location where you are planning; always to be found in the location where you are doing the post-mortem.

IDENTIFYING CHARACTERISTICS: Grey feathers, long beak, the belief that all events are predictable.

Look at these fucking idiots

CONSUMMATE FALCON

The consummate falcon's distinctive cry is a declaration that it does not even own a television, and that only sheep would watch something as unchallenging and low-brow as *The Bachelor*.

HABITAT: Can usually be found watching *The Bachelor* and then tweeting angrily about it afterwards. From a pseudonymous account, naturally.

IDENTIFYING CHARACTERISTICS: An encyclopedic knowledge of all previous contestants on *The Bachelor* and what they're up to right now.

NOT TODAY

SPOTTED DO-NOTHING

The spotted do-nothing is aghast at the state of the modern world and wishes we could all just go back to the way things were when it was young.

HABITAT: Often found moaning in the comments under political articles, though they also appear with regularity wherever millennials are mentioned.

IDENTIFYING CHARACTERISTICS: No conception of their part in making the world worse, and no suggestions for how to make it better.

THAT'S

FUCKED

SNITCHES
GET STITCHES

*Make
it end*

Here comes bullshit

FORECAST CARDINAL

This bird has the fortunate ability to see what's coming, but an unfortunate lack of ambition to do anything about it.

HABITAT: Cable news panel shows, dark web internet forums, and Thanksgiving dinner with the extended family.

IDENTIFYING CHARACTERISTICS: Their bookshelves are lined with dystopian fiction, but they can't be bothered to get the tinfoil from the kitchen to line their hat.

Look at this clusterfuck

I have feelings

Fuck emotions

Keep it in your pants

APPRAISING BLUEBIRD

If you don't want the appraising bluebird's opinion on something, you should not show that something to the appraising bluebird.

HABITAT: For some incomprehensible reason, people constantly seek out the appraising bluebird. It doesn't hide, but it sure as hell doesn't have a neon sign by its nest that says, "I WANT TO HEAR YOUR HOT TAKES."

IDENTIFYING CHARACTERISTICS: While its victims wish it were not the case, the appraising bluebird feels no obligation to be kind when replying to an unsolicted opinion.

Fuck off

DEPARTURE MARTIN

Departure martins will tell you when it is time to go, where you
should go, and what you should do once you get there.

HABITAT: It is not generally welcome in one's living room, but on the
other hand it will garner applause when it has told off a particularly
obnoxious patron in the line at Starbucks.

IDENTIFYING CHARACTERISTICS: Good sense, strong moral fibre, and a
complete inability to leave shit alone.

Shut the fuck up

BULL SHIT

LISTEN TO MY OPINIONS

TUMULTUOUS TERN

Like some kind of verbal fire hose, the tumultuous tern spews out an endless stream of poorly researched invective.

HABITAT: The official bird of Twitter.

IDENTIFYING CHARACTERISTICS: Compact, loud, unable to process or synthesise feedback and counterarguments. Most important, it is blue.

HOLY SHIT

I NEED
CAFFEINE

VIRTUOUS VULTURE

This vulture moves at a glacial pace that makes one wonder if it is still alive, but then it suddenly snaps into action at the first sign that someone, somewhere, has made a mistake. Correcting a hapless idiot is the virtuous vulture's raison d'être, and in the same way that a hammer treats all problems as nails, the virtuous vulture views all other living creatures as hapless idiots.

HABITAT: Wherever you find them, you don't want to be there anymore.

IDENTIFYING CHARACTERISTICS: When a virtuous vulture approaches, a kind of static energy crackles in the air. If you can learn to identify this sensation, you can get the fuck out of there while there's still time.

WE ALL
SAW YOU
FUCK
THAT UP

I'm

already

drunk

WHEN WILL IT ALL FUCKING END?

YOU HAVE A HIGH OPINION OF YOURSELF FOR A GIGANTIC FUCKING DUNCE

I SEE WE'RE BACK TO EATING OUR OWN POOP

I'M NOT LAUGHING, FUCKWEED

YOU DIM MOTHERFUCKER, SCIENCE IS REAL

COMPETENT OWL

Competent owls hold the mistaken belief that being right allows one to be a dickhead.

HABITAT: Causing more harm than good in arguments with complete strangers.

IDENTIFYING CHARACTERISTICS: Righteous anger that the massive blind spot around their own behaviour causes others to ignore their message.

THE WORLD IS A SHITBARGE

HIPSTER PELICAN

"There's a real magic to vintage vinyl," the hipster pelican tells you. "Decades of experiences and emotions have been absorbed right into the LP; you can't get that from a streaming service."

HABITAT: Probably at the vegan, locally-sourced juice bar.

IDENTIFYING CHARACTERISTICS: Carefully coiffed plumage – plenty above and below the face, but absolutely none on the sides – and carefully selected items in its nest, all curated to tell you a story about how much this bird cares.

HONESTLY, I CAN'T
TAKE ANY MORE
OF THIS SHIT

JUST FUCKING
GOOGLE IT

PG 63

YOU ASSBAG

VITUPERATIVE LARK

This is one of those birds that you don't see until it is too late.

HABITAT: You wish you knew, just so you could avoid it.

IDENTIFYING CHARACTERISTICS: Swooping down from a great height, it lets out an ear-splitting screech right before it rips off your wig and carries it back to its nest.

THE CORRECT ANSWER
IS FUCK OFF

I HAVE NEVER MET
A PROUDER IDIOT

SAY THAT SHIT TO MY FACE

COMBED GOSHAWK

The problem with insulting a combed goshawk is that it will find out about it and confront you in the most uncomfortable way possible.

HABITAT: Always where other people are around, because it isn't really humiliation if it happens in private.

IDENTIFYING CHARACTERISTICS: Loud voice, unyielding glare, endless patience.

TAKE SOME RESPONSIBILITY FOR YOUR BULLSHIT

INCULPATE CHICKEN

Like the proverbial sparrow with a machine gun, the inculpate chicken is small but dangerous.

HABITAT: Wherever there is blame to be laid.

IDENTIFYING CHARACTERISTICS: Most easily found by following the trail of bewildered dudes lying on the ground, trying to process being held accountable for something for the first time in their lives.

GET
FUUUUCKED

I AM FULLY
AWARE OF HOW
FUCKING AWESOME
I AM

THIS IS A BIG FRIGGING WASTE OF ENERGY

OBVIATED WARBLER

While some would call its lifestyle choice "sloth," the obviated warbler prefers to call it "a differentiated set of priorities."

HABITAT: Anywhere, as long as there is Netflix.

IDENTIFYING CHARACTERISTICS: A distinctive, keening song that it sings from sunrise to sunset while staying in the same position.

WHERE IS YOUR FUCKING BRAIN?

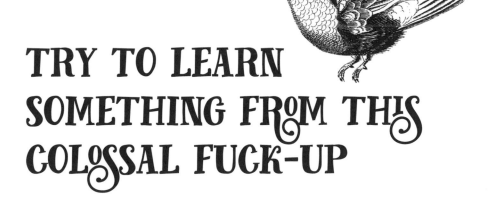

TRY TO LEARN SOMETHING FROM THIS COLOSSAL FUCK-UP

THIS IS SOME GRADE-SCHOOL BULLSHIT

MATURE BUZZARD

The mature buzzard is here to remind you of what you should and should not be doing, based on the elapsed time since your birth.

HABITAT: Generally found where there is fun to be had, discouraging it.

IDENTIFYING CHARACTERISTICS: It wears a button-down shirt with a tie; don't listen to anything it has to say.

EAT
FARTS

IS THIS NEW BULLSHIT OR JUST THE SAME OLD BULLSHIT?

ABSTRUSE HERON

This small, irritating bird asks questions that it already knows the answer to.

HABITAT: The back of your mind.

IDENTIFYING CHARACTERISTICS: Persistence, nagging, sudden appearances when things are going well.

CAN THIS
SHIT BE
SOMEONE
ELSE'S
PROBLEM?

YOU ARE NOT
CAPABLE OF
PRODUCING A
USEFUL RESULT

OBJECTIVELY SPEAKING, THIS IS BULLSHIT

I LIVE IN A FUCKING TREE, IDIOT

GO AWAY, DICKBAG

DOMINION TEAL

The dominion teal is notably territorial but determines its territory on a whim.

HABITAT: Today it might be this patch of grass by the edge of the pond, and tomorrow it might be the fourth barstool from the left. But no matter where it decides is its territory, you are the interloper, even if you've been sitting on the stool for the last hour.

IDENTIFYING CHARACTERISTICS: Avoid making direct eye contact with a dominion teal.

FUCK THIS SHIT, I'M OUT OF HERE

I HAVE PUT UP WITH ENOUGH BULLSHIT FOR THREE LIFETIMES

THIS IS SOME BAROQUE DOGSHIT

DISCERNING BUFFLEHEAD

While the discerning bufflehead isn't going to put up with your shit, it does appreciate the amount of effort that went into it. The bufflehead merely wishes you had put that effort into your job instead.

HABITAT: Sitting directly across from you during your annual review.

IDENTIFYING CHARACTERISTICS: A lot of sighing.

YOU SELF-IMPORTANT
PIECE OF SHIT

SANDWICH TERN

While most bird enthusiasts assume that the sandwich tern
was named for the food item that it frequently steals from
picnickers, it was actually named for the Earl of Sandwich,
a self-important piece of shit.

WHY AM I
SO FUCKING
UNLOVABLE?

GET
OFF MY
LAWN

THAT'S A BIG FUCKING NOPE

JUST FUCKING GREAT

SARDONIC JAY

With a longer lifespan than most birds, the sardonic jay tends to become jaded as it ages. At some point, everyone assumes that any expression of happiness or enthusiasm from the sardonic jay must be sarcasm, and after a while even the jay itself is unsure. Maybe it was never happy at all.

HABITAT: A home that was expensive – that should be a sign it's a good house, right? This is a nice place to live, right? God, why did I spend all this money on this house?

IDENTIFYING CHARACTERISTICS: A quiver at the edge of its smile.

I CAN'T DEAL WITH YOUR SHIT TODAY

THAT'S NOT HOW REALITY WORKS, DUMBSHIT

NOW WOULD
BE A GREAT
TIME FOR
YOU TO SHUT
YOUR FUCKING
MOUTH

ARE YOU
FUCKING
SERIOUS?

TIME FOR A VACATION FROM YOUR BULLSHIT

FALTER OWL

The falter owl is driven by an astute sense of self-preservation. When it finds itself surrounded by other owls that are mentally or physically draining, it will frequently disappear for an hour.

HABITAT: If you haven't seen it for a while, sometimes you can find it in the bathroom.

IDENTIFYING CHARACTERISTICS: Sometimes it says it forgot to get something from the store; sometimes it remembers that it left the oven on; and sometimes it just has to take this important call even though no one heard its phone buzz.

YOU ARE AN IRRESPONSIBLE CRAP PILE

PRECIPITOUS EAGLE

Charming, fun to be around, generous with its time and energy – everyone loves the precipitous eagle, at least at first.

HABITAT: It probably still lives in the basement of its parents' house.

IDENTIFYING CHARACTERISTICS: It can be hard to tell a precipitous eagle from a run-of-the-mill eagle until you've been around it for a while – the pattern of late arrivals, broken promises, and unfinished projects takes time to recognise. But once you do recognise it, you can bake it into your plans and avoid a lot of messy family drama.

WELL,
AREN'T YOU
HOT SHIT

I DIDN'T GET
OUT OF BED TO
DEAL WITH
THIS BULLSHIT

BETTER LUCK NEXT TIME, FUCKNUTS

OVERBEARING HERON

This heron's primary source of joy is the misfortune of others. And while it always feels like their comeuppance is just around the corner, it never seems to arrive.

HABITAT: You'll be having a perfectly ordinary conversation, and the overbearing heron will swoop in: "Did you hear about Sharon?" it asks in a way that you know means it is about to tell you about Sharon.

IDENTIFYING CHARACTERISTICS: Through some alchemical combination of tone of voice and body language, this bird is able to convey "this is a secret" in a voice loud enough for everyone to hear.

I AM SO THANKFUL
THAT YOU ARE HERE TO
EXPLAIN MY JOB TO ME

APPRENTICE EIDER

The apprentice eider is a formidable predator from an early age.

HABITAT: If it isn't at its desk, check by the water cooler.

IDENTIFYING CHARACTERISTICS: A thousand-yard stare that cuts into your soul, a snarky attitude, and the ability to turn any offer of assistance into an insult.

FUCK YOU,
I'M HILARIOUS

I AM SO FUCKING HIGH

AREN'T YOU A FANCY MOTHERFUCKER

REGARD'S FLAMINGO

Stemming from a deep lack of self-esteem, the regard's flamingo nitpicks any outward display of success by other birds. At first this seems reasonable – you ask yourself, "Am I being ostentatious?" You stop wearing your nice watch to work. But listen, you worked hard for that watch. Does it bring you some small amount of joy during the day? Then wear the goddamn watch.

HABITAT: Always in the orbit of successful people.

IDENTIFYING CHARACTERISTICS: Great-looking shoes that they will stress to you they got on sale.

GOOD LUCK WITH YOUR BULLSHIT

FUCK ALL OF THAT

CALM
YOUR SHIT
DOWN AND
TRY AGAIN

FEMINISM
IS FOR
EVERYONE,
DIPSHIT

FUCK WORK

Listen, none of us wants to be here today. You muttering about it isn't helping. Let's all get shit done until 3 p.m. and then have a "team meeting" where we just do Twitter on our phones for a couple of hours and then we can get the fuck out of here without losing our health insurance.

IT'S TOO EARLY IN THE MORNING FOR ME TO TRY

AMBITIOUS SHRIKE

There is always something impeding the ambitious shrike. It could be a hair appointment, or a recall on its car, or a general distrust of Wednesdays in the middle of the month. Whatever it is, overcoming it is virtually impossible.

HABITAT: At the bottom of the stack ranking, wondering how it scored so low.

IDENTIFYING CHARACTERISTICS: A truly astounding ability to describe things in a way that puts all blame and responsibility onto the nebulous energies of the universe.

CAN YOU GO
BE A FUCKING
GARBAGE PERSON
SOMEWHERE ELSE,
PLEASE?

YOU ARE A
SPECTACULAR
AMOUNT OF
WRONG

WELCOME TO MUTESVILLE, FUCKO

OBLIVIOUS PHEASANT

The whole point of muting someone on social media is so that you don't hear from them anymore, but they have no idea and keep hooting into the void. When you announce it, they know you're not listening and turn their unwanted attention to another victim. Please, for the rest of our sakes, don't tell them that you're muting them.

YOU CAN GO EAT A DICK
AS FAR AS I'M CONCERNED

I'M GLAD
I'M NOT
THE ONLY
ONE DEALING
WITH THIS
SHIT

WELL, THAT WAS A FUCKING WASTE OF RESOURCES

HUSBAND OWL

No one is more fiercely protective of corporate assets than the husband owl. The Post-it note rationing system, the binder re-use policy, and the company-wide maximum on the number of colours in a printed document were all the brilliant efforts of the husband owl.

HABITAT: In the stockroom, wondering why they cannot find love.

IDENTIFYING CHARACTERISTICS: A photographic memory, but only for the pettiest of things.

HOLD
ON TO
YOUR
SHIT

GODDAMN FUCKING SHIT

I'VE PASSED
BETTER IDEAS
OUT OF MY
BUTTHOLE

THE FUCK YOU SAY?

UGH

UNIDENTIFIED SPECIMEN

While little is known about this as-yet unidentified bird, it is clear that its bones were picked clean by life.

FRANKLY, I EXPECTED MORE

Part Two

WATER BIRDS

Found in ponds, lakes, and rivers, water birds frequently have words for cottagers and outdoorsmen – and those words are, "Take your $800 hiking boots and your fucking survival pants from the internet back to the city, chump."

EVERYBODY FUCK OFF
FOR A WHILE

HERMIT SANDPIPER

The best way to connect with a hermit sandpiper is by text message, even if it lives next door.

HABITAT: While it tends to nest in accessible areas, it actively avoids contact with humans.

IDENTIFYING CHARACTERISTICS: You'd have to find one in the first place.

HERE IS THE VALIDATION YOU CRAVE

BULLSEYE GULL

The bullseye gull's detailed understanding of what makes a person tick allows it to deliver laser-guided criticism directly into the heart of its prey. Do not tell it about your childhood, your insecurities, your hobbies, your career – hell, just walk in the other direction if you see one coming.

HABITAT: Once you've encountered a bullseye gull, it lives in your head forever.

IDENTIFYING CHARACTERISTICS: Eyes that see into your soul; razor-sharp claws (at least, metaphorically).

I CALLED YOUR MOTHER
TO COME PICK YOU UP

WHITE-BELLIED COSSET

The white-bellied cosset takes charge of younger birds in
its orbit, teaching them about etiquette, how to save money
for a house, workplace norms, and more, regardless of the
desires of the younger birds.

HABITAT: A cubicle full of Beanie Babies and cut-out
magazine pictures.

IDENTIFYING CHARACTERISTICS: If you cross a white-bellied cosset, expect
that it will call your parents and express disappointment in you.

YOU ARE VERY BRAVE TO MAKE SUCH A GIGANTIC ASS OF YOURSELF

RED-WINGED DEHORT

Where other birds offer encouraging words, the red-winged dehort focuses on the worst-case scenario.

HABITAT: Karaoke bars, open mics, presentations, the dance floor.

IDENTIFYING CHARACTERISTICS: You can tell the red-winged dehort is near because it emits an unpleasant, damp sensation that blankets the area.

DO YOU THINK I'M A FUCKING IDIOT?

HAUGHTY PENGUIN

"He who smelt it dealt it" is a childish expression with limited application to adult life, though it does neatly characterise the protestations of the haughty penguin.

HABITAT: Wherever the fucking idiots hang out these days.

IDENTIFYING CHARACTERISTICS: Keen sense of smell, peculiar speckle pattern on its belly, and an inability to distinguish when it is, in fact, being a fucking idiot.

WAS BEING A DIPSHIT A JOB REQUIREMENT?

THANKS FOR NOTHING, FUCKFACE

WHY DID YOU WAIT UNTIL
THE LAST FUCKING MINUTE?

YOUR INPUT IS NOT REQUIRED

DON'T MAKE ME FUCK UP
ALL YOUR SHIT

GO FUCK A TREE

HAVE SOME FUCKING WINE

PRETEND I'M STILL LISTENING

I DO NOT WANT TO HEAR
YOUR FUCKING LIFE STORY

SMOOTH-BELLIED EXASPERATOR

The motionless, dead eyes of the smooth-bellied exasperator are
at odds with its never-silent mouth.

HABITAT: Found at parties, asking open-ended questions out of
a sense of duty.

IDENTIFYING CHARACTERISTICS: A total lack of interest in you, your
employment, your hobbies, or your family.

PRETTY SURE YOU
MADE THAT SHIT UP

MAYBE
TOMORROW
YOU'LL BE
LESS OF A
SHITHEAD

FUCK THE OUTDOORS

BUFF PETREL

The buff petrel is oblivious to the visual and auditory cues that you do not wish to go on a hike with it. "It will be fun," it keeps saying. You know that this is not true.

HABITAT: If it's not halfway up the side of a mountain or deep in an old-growth forest, you can find it in the sporting goods store, buying more carabiners.

IDENTIFYING CHARACTERISTICS: Clad in moisture-wicking, high-tech fabrics and sporting multiple exercise trackers.

TURN
AROUND AND
FUCK RIGHT OFF

GIMME A
FUCKIN'
BREAK

FUCK THIS SHITAPALOOZA

DEPRECATING GOOSE

Experienced birders know to avoid the deprecating goose – it's territorial and aggressive, and its bite leaves a mark for weeks.

HABITAT: No matter where you put your tent, you've just put it beside a nest of deprecating geese. Get out the topical antiseptic – you're gonna need it.

IDENTIFYING CHARACTERISTICS: Did it bite you? Yes, you spotted one. You're lucky to still have all of your fingers.

GET
YOUR SHIT
TOGETHER

LOOK AT THIS
GODDAMN
SHITSHOW

WHERE'S THE FUCKING GIN?

ENLIGHTENED GOOSANDER

This flexible, mellow water bird takes the entire world with a pinch of salt around the top of a shot glass.

HABITAT: Found in almost every climate, making friends with the bartender.

IDENTIFYING CHARACTERISTICS: You could argue that more of the buttons on its shirt could be done up, but somehow it's making it work.

WHAT THE FUCK IS WRONG WITH PEOPLE?

PLEASE TELL ME MORE ABOUT MY OWN GODDAMN EXPERIENCES

I AM GOING TO FUCK OFF NOW

RECOGNISANT DUCK

The recognisant duck is keenly attuned to the emotional make-up of a room, and therefore knows exactly when it's time to take off.

HABITAT: It left the party a vital fifteen minutes before you did.

IDENTIFYING CHARACTERISTICS: It leaves a trail of quizzical "She was just here!" exclamations in its wake.

I HAVE NO FURTHER INTEREST
IN YOUR BULLSHIT

CAN YOU FUCK OFF AND NEVER
UN-FUCK OFF?

EAT WOODCHIPS, FUCKSTICK

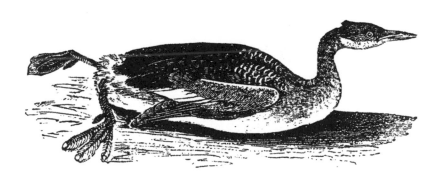

GET BENT

YOU ARE FUCKING RIDICULOUS

SMEW

The smew is possibly the most disagreeable family of birds. The expression "do not fuck with a smew" is folk wisdom rooted in fact.

HABITAT: Often found in executive suites, penthouse apartments, or Congress.

IDENTIFYING CHARACTERISTICS: While they come in many sizes, shapes, and colours, smews are all aggressive, territorial, and strangely attuned to your insecurities.

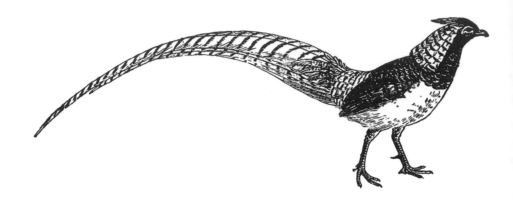

CAN YOUR BULLSHIT WAIT
UNTIL TOMORROW?

DECAMPING GULL

It's 4:52 p.m. Why are you bringing me this now?

I'M SURE THAT SOUNDED GREAT IN YOUR HEAD

REMIND ME: ARE YOU A FUCKING IMBECILE?

PALPABLE RANGER

A vital part of our ecosystem, the palpable ranger provides an important public service: asking the questions that we all know the answer to.

HABITAT: Can be found in guest columns, talking-head TV spots or, most stressfully, conducting your job interview.

IDENTIFYING CHARACTERISTICS: It always seems to be much more prepared than you are.

DO NOT CARE, GOODBYE

IT MUST BE DICKHEAD SEASON

BALLS

ROYAL SWIFT

Known for its majesty and grace, the royal swift makes only a single sound: a breathy, frustrated release.

HABITAT: Facing the television, watching the news.

IDENTIFYING CHARACTERISTICS: The royal swift will freeze in place, eyes locked on the screen, unable to move or change the channel. Shimmering lines of heat radiate from its head. A pulsing vein, usually on the temple or neck, appears dangerously close to rupturing. But the royal swift will keep watching right up until its head explodes.

ME SAYING I
LIKE SOMETHING
IS NOT AN
INVITATION
TO A FUCKING
DEBATE

I DIDN'T LISTEN TO YOUR VOICEMAIL
BECAUSE WE LIVE IN THE GODDAMN
TWENTY-FIRST CENTURY

MAYBE TRY NOT BEING A DICKHEAD

COUNSELLOR SWALLOW

The counsellor swallow offers up what should be obvious advice that, nevertheless, people still need.

HABITAT: Once they lived in newsprint columns, but these days they are more commonly found on blogs.

IDENTIFYING CHARACTERISTICS: A surprised or perplexed expression: "Isn't this just common sense?"

What is this shit?

MENDACIOUS RAVEN

The mendacious raven knows exactly what this shit is; its cawing
is just an attempt to get you to interact with it. And don't get me
wrong, it can be fun for a while. Just stop before you also become
a mendacious raven.

HABITAT: There's one in every office.

IDENTIFYING CHARACTERISTICS: If they bite you, you'll turn into
a complaining, feathered mess when the moon is full or when
prime-time network TV is on.

Fuck This

Bleah

This place is bullshit

MOANING VIREO

If it isn't the venue, it's the DJ. If it isn't the DJ, it's the clientele. Or the lighting. Or the decor. Or the quality of the alcohol served at the bar. Or the softness of the towels in the bathroom. Or any other excuse to not have a good time.

HABITAT: In your social circle, though you're wondering why you continue to invite them out with you.

IDENTIFYING CHARACTERISTICS: Like a whirling vortex that consumes fun and enjoyment.

Go to the fucking library

LITERATE PLOVER

Let's be real: there's no way you found this book at the
library. Still, libraries are fucking awesome; you should go
to them and get some books that aren't just a bunch of
pictures of birds and swear words.

*We both know
that's bullshit*

Blah blah blah

CRUSHED TURACO

The turaco has sprained its indignation muscle, and all it has left is a sad kind of resignation. It isn't quite nihilism, but it involves a lot of Netflix and booze.

HABITAT: This bed is comfortable. . . . Why would it get out of this comfortable bed?

IDENTIFYING CHARACTERISTICS: A collection of blankets and pillows, sometimes arranged into a fort.

This is my surprised face

OSTENTATIOUS OSPREY

This bird is in a constant state of discomfort for the sake of fashion.

HABITAT: You can find it trying not to trip over its own feet on the short walk between its luxury car and the mall.

IDENTIFYING CHARACTERISTICS: Absurdly gigantic sunglasses, a watch the size of a can of tuna, and shoes too impractical to wear for any length of time.

I'm fancy

Fight me

TRUCULENT HAWK

It wasn't you, don't worry about it. The hawk just
wants to have an argument. It lives a small, lonely
life and thinks that it will feel better if it is able to
hurt someone else, verbally or physically, to show
that it isn't at the bottom of the food chain. You can
walk away with your head held high, knowing that is
exactly where it is and where it deserves to be.

HABITAT: Bars, clubs, Twitter.

IDENTIFYING CHARACTERISTICS: If you look into its eyes
for long enough, that defiance melts into depression.

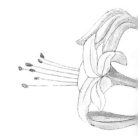

I'm done
with your shit

YOU'VE CORNERED THE
MARKET ON STUPID SHIT

THIS IS A FUCKING GARBAGE FIRE

WELL, AREN'T YOU JUST THE KING OF SHIT MOUNTAIN

ESTIMATE'S WIGEON

Your accomplishments, aspirations, and accolades mean nothing to an estimate's wigeon. The more you talk about yourself, the less it likes you.

HABITAT: Sometimes it contributes unsolicited reviews of your work on Twitter that you are able to talk your publisher into using on the back cover of your book.

IDENTIFYING CHARACTERISTICS: Impeccable credentials; no sense of humour.

N🦆PE

YOU ARE BY FAR THE STUPIDEST FUCKER
I HAVE EVER MET

I AM IGNORING YOUR SHIT

WHY ARE YOU STILL TALKING?

SNUB GULL

Life has piled bullshit up in front of the snub gull, from its terrible
name to its habitat in the swamp. And while the snub gull is
generally patient, at some point everything becomes too much.
If you're lucky, it will just walk away from you. If you're unlucky,
you'll lose a finger first.

HABITAT: The shitty bottom end of shit marsh, at the base of shit hill,
shaded by shit trees. But at least it has a partial view of shit lake.

IDENTIFYING CHARACTERISTICS: It appears to not be registering
any of the shit around it, giving no visible reaction to the
growing shitpile. Then all of a sudden, it'll shiver. If you see
the shiver, it's too late for you.

OH, HONEY, NO

DIAL THAT SHIT WAY BACK

FUCK THIS, I'M GOING BACK TO BED

I DO NOT NEED YOUR SHIT

WHADDUP, WIENERS?

SHINDIG'S MALLARD

Because it is inappropriately jocular and abusive in an upbeat way, it can be confusing to encounter a shindig's mallard. Were you just insulted? Should you be upset? Why are you laughing?

HABITAT: Near the water cooler or some other vital area of the workplace that you can't completely avoid.

IDENTIFYING CHARACTERISTICS: A wide, toothy grin and the smell of cheap aftershave.

TOODLE-OO, FUCKFACE

IS IT DUMBFUCK O'CLOCK
ALREADY?

WHAT ARE YOU, THE FUCKING GENITALS POLICE?

BAILIWICK GULL

The bailiwick gulls may have moved their meetings out of dimly-lit church basements and into Facebook groups, but their sense of morality has remained firmly in the 1950s.

HABITAT: Cable news shows, opinion columns, and other places where impotent rage is found.

IDENTIFYING CHARACTERISTICS: An obsession with the way that other people live and the need to exert some form of control that it clearly doesn't feel in its own life, often coupled with an intense fear of what happens in public washrooms.

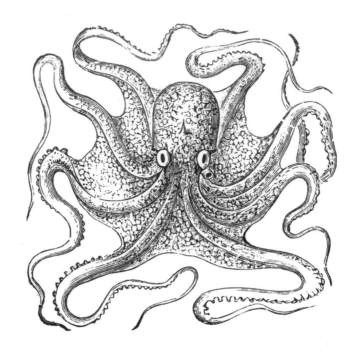

WELL, THIS IS FUCKING
AWKWARD

THAT IS SOME FUCKED-UP SHIT

STUNNED GUILLEMOT

At some point, these waterfowl just gave up trying to understand
the world around them.

HABITAT: Near Wi-Fi and a power outlet.

IDENTIFYING CHARACTERISTICS: Glassy-eyed, they acknowledge that we
are in a terrible hellscape and then continue to binge-watch Netflix.

℧UR EXPECTATION℧
FOR YOU WERE LOW,
BUT HOLY FUCK

EVALUATIVE MERGANSER

This invasive species wraps itself in the protective cloak of "constructive criticism" and "feedback" but is more interested in point-scoring and its general feeling of superiority. Once there's an evaluative merganser on your management team, it's probably time to burn the whole thing down and start again.

HABITAT: Always in their office, and you have to come to them.

IDENTIFYING CHARACTERISTICS: A commitment to the numbers, because if they can make the numbers, who gives a shit about how they accomplished it?

TODAY'S GOLD
MEDAL FOR
BEING THE
STUPIDEST
GOES TO YOU

I BET THIS
PROBLEM
WILL GO AWAY
IF WE HAVE
MORE FUCKING
MEETINGS

GET OUT OF MY FUCKING FACE

IRATE STORK

These birds are associated with the delivery of babies in folklore,
but in real life they should never be put anywhere near the extreme
challenge to one's self-restraint known as a human child.

HABITAT: Frustratingly, these birds prefer to nest near the moat
of the fairy-tale castle.

IDENTIFYING CHARACTERISTICS: Long legs and necks.

YOU ARE TESTING MY PATIENCE

WELCOME
TO HELL

ARE YOU
FUCKING
KIDDING ME?

WHO FUCKING CARES?

THIS SHIT AGAIN

YOU CAN ALL FUCK OFF UNTIL MONDAY

REASONABLE PIGEON

This bird walks the fine line between work/life balance and not giving a shit. Though if it gets all its work done, does it really matter?

HABITAT: Building Lego with the kids.

IDENTIFYING CHARACTERISTICS: The ability to disconnect from every contact method and vanish from its desk in the space between 4:52 and 5:00 p.m.

HOW ABOUT SOME FUCKING DECORUM

COURTEOUS DUCK

Policing your tone with no regard for its own, this duck is simply trying to derail you. Minute-to-minute reality does not apply; yesterday was 1,000 years ago in another era and all those people are dead now. Every word of every interaction is parsed in a vacuum. Context not only doesn't matter, it is actively shunned.

HABITAT: Wedged firmly in the middle of the pathetic, shouty mess that passes for political discourse these days.

IDENTIFYING CHARACTERISTICS: A tenuous grasp of grammar and punctuation combined with an unearned confidence that it is "winning."

LOOK AT ME NOT GIVING A SHIT

FULMINATING GREBE

Methinks the bird doth protest too much, or however that saying goes. The fulminating grebe loudly, defiantly proclaims that it does not care but then retreats to its nest to cry.

HABITAT: The Twitter mentions of people it had to seek out in order to read their opinions so they could not care about them.

IDENTIFYING CHARACTERISTICS: Loud voice, red-rimmed eyes, despair.

FUCK ALL YOU GUYS

INFELICITOUS DUCK

Known for inappropriately expressing its emotions, this duck cares strongly about its family and friends. No matter how often it tells you to fuck off, if you actually fucked off it would be heartbroken.

HABITAT: Wherever you are, telling you to fuck off.

IDENTIFYING CHARACTERISTICS: The infelicitous duck is very good at hugging. The hugs just come with inappropriate whispers in your ear.

SAYONARA, MOTHERFUCKERS

Acknowledgements

This book would not have been possible without the following people.

Nolan, Oliver, Theo, and Vanessa: thank you for putting up with all of the terrible ideas that led to this good one. Vanessa, I'm sorry about the three-foot print that says "EAT FARTS" on Nolan's wall. Nolan, I hope you like your print.

Carrie from the Audubon Society: your email changed everything.

Beth from Unbound: thank you for pushing me to do this.

Thomas Bewick: you are at the same time a great artist and also the grumpiest motherfucker who ever wrote a book about birds. You are an inspiration.

An extra-special thank you to the 1,600 Legendary Bird Friends whose support made this book possible.

A Note on the Author

Aaron Reynolds is a humorist, professional speaker, and the man behind the @EffinBirds and @swear_trek Twitter accounts. When he's not on Twitter, you can find him producing a series of podcasts and at Comic-Cons dressed as George Lucas. He has been a baseball writer, a fine art printer, and a mall Santa Claus photographer. Aaron was raised in Mississauga, Canada, a suburb where they cut down all the trees and named the streets after them. He currently splits his time between Toronto and Ottawa.

The End

All rights reserved.
Published in the United States by Ten Speed Press, an imprint of Random House,
a division of Penguin Random House LLC, New York.
www.tenspeed.com

Ten Speed Press and the Ten Speed Press colophon are registered trademarks
of Penguin Random House LLC.

Published in the United Kingdom by Unbound, London, www.unbound.com.

Internal and cover illustrations originally published in BIRDS OF AMERICA
by John James Audubon, HISTORY OF BRITISH BIRDS, Vols. I and II by
Thomas Berwick and the Knight's Pictorial Museum of Animated Nature series.

Library of Congress Cataloging-in-Publication Data
Names: Reynolds, Aaron, 1975– author.
Title: Effin' birds : a field guide to identification / Aaron Reynolds.
Description: First edition. | New York : Ten Speed Press, [2019]
Identifiers: LCCN 2019021684| ISBN 9781984856289 (hardcover) |
    ISBN 9781984856296 (ebook)
Subjects: LCSH: Birds—Identification. | Birds—Humor.
Classification: LCC QL673 .R49 2019 | DDC 598—dc23 LC record available
at https://lccn.loc.gov/2019021684

Hardcover ISBN: 978-1-9848-5628-9
ebook ISBN: 978-1-9848-5629-6

Printed in China

Text design by carrdesignstudio.com
Cover design by Lizzie Allen, based on a design by Mecob

10 9

First US Edition